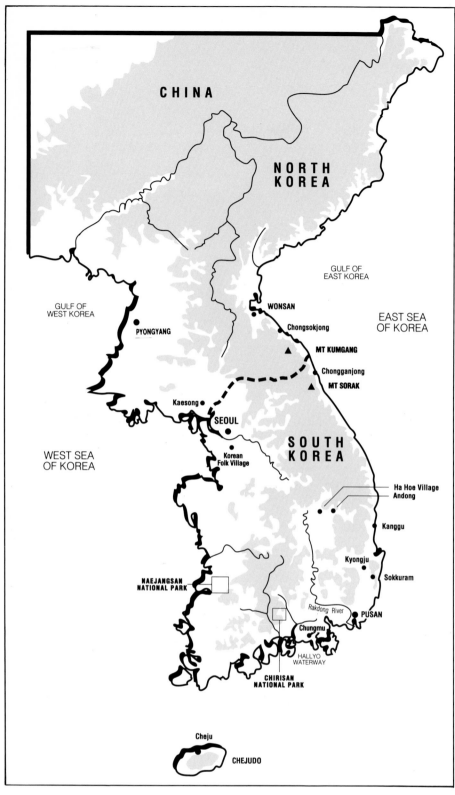

Jacket: Master of Ceremonies, traditional Korean wedding

End Papers: 1000 Buddhas of the Life of Buddha as a child — Chickchisa

1. *Half Title:* Traditional symbol indicating harmony of man/earth/heaven

2. *Previous page* Tying cabbages —
Suwon Folk Village, South of Seoul — South Korea

3. Statue of Kim Il Sung, Pyongyang — North Korea

4. *Following page* Early morning, Andong region — South Korea

KOREA

LAND OF THE MORNING CALM

Text *Chong-Sik Lee*
Photography Mike Langford

UNIVERSE

Published in the United States of America in 1988 by Universe Books, 381 Park Avenue South, New York, N.Y. 10016

© 1988 by Chong-Sik Lee
© photographs by Mike Langford 1988

88 89 90 91 92 / 10 9 8 7 6 5 4 3 2 1

Printed in Hong Kong by South China Printing Company
Typeset by Post Typesetters, Brisbane, Queensland, Australia

ISBN 0-87663-693-8

Designed & produced for the Publishers by
J.M. McGregor Pty Ltd, PO Box 6990, Gold Coast Mail Centre Qld. 4217

5. Bullrushes at sunset, Island of Kanghwado — South Korea

진 Few Koreans today realise that their land once abounded with tigers — the black striped Siberian variety that adorn many Korean paintings. Even fewer Koreans know that only a hundred years ago, such tigers roamed the streets of Seoul at night in search of prey. It is no accident that the mascot of the 1988 International Olympics is a tiger... the friendly and smiling kind! Back then it was not just tigers the nights brought. One well-known missionary to Korea recorded that she lay awake during a summer night in Seoul certain that she heard the stealthy, heavy tread of one of these creatures in her room: a leopard had been seen in her neighbourhood a few days earlier. That was in the year 1888.

Nor can Koreans today easily visualise how the capital looked a hundred years ago. Foreigners described the city as a vast bed of mushrooms because no Korean house stood more than one storey high, roofed with either thatch, straw or tiles.

Seoul has changed so much since those days that now it is not very different from many metropolitan cities found in the West. The city's main thoroughfare is lined with skyscrapers, hotels, department stores and apartment buildings. The narrow streets and alleys of old are replaced by boulevards jammed with cars and buses. Some Koreans feel that the change of pace has been too fast...

But even now one finds some familiar landmarks here and there. The old palaces remain intact, even refurbished. The old stone structure that at one time housed the Japanese colonial government, badly damaged during the Second World War, is restored and now houses the National Museum. The old Seoul Railroad Station hasn't changed much either. But such landmarks are few and rare.

As for Pyongyang, now the capital of North Korea, only a few landmarks remain. Were it not for familiar rivers and hills, even the old residents would be unable to find their bearings in the park-like city which the Communist regime rebuilt from scratch after the Korean war.

The countryside of Korea has changed too. Purplish-grey thatched roofs that for centuries represented the Korean countryside are replaced by more colourful Western-style houses. The North Korean countryside is dotted with apartment buildings, something unknown before 1953. Television antennas are everywhere, and farmers have long forgotten the days when they had to do without electricity. Industrial parks dot the South Korean countryside where there was once nothing but rice paddies with plough-pulling oxen.

Just forty years ago, in February 1948, the American General Charles G. Helmick declared his prognosis for Korea — a prognosis that was far from optimistic. Helmick served in Seoul as Deputy Military Governor of the U.S. occupation forces in South Korea after Korea was liberated from Japan in 1945. Now Korea was about to become an independent nation.

Helmick told his colleagues in Washington D.C., "Korea can never attain a high standard of living. There are virtually no Koreans with the technical training and experience required to take advantage of Korea's resources and effect an improvement over its present rice-economy status."

He also predicted that when the U.S. occupation forces withdrew and stopped sending in the supplies that South Korea needed, it would be reduced to a "bull cart" economy, and some nine million non-food producers would face starvation. The General gave little chance for South Korea to survive, and few disagreed with him at that time.

The situation looked even more bleak in the summer of 1950 when the Korean War broke out. Cities and villages became battlefronts and most buildings were destroyed by bombardments from both sides. Tens of thousands of soldiers and civilians — both North and South Korean — were killed and injured. Those who survived had little hope for a decent standard of living; the nation remained divided as the two hostile regimes confronted each other with large armies.

Helmick would have been surprised, to say the least, to see how Korea has developed to become the nation it is today. The days of "rice-economy" are long gone. Korea still produces rice, of course, but it no longer depends on it for its survival.

South Korea produces and exports automobiles by the thousands. Gone are the days when Koreans flattened cast-off oil drums to build buses that ran on rebuilt truck engines. Off assembly lines roll modern buses of every type. Korean shipyards build the largest oil tankers and ships the world has ever known. North Korea, with a head start in its development, also shows off a great number of industrial complexes.

The lack of technically trained people is no longer a problem. When Korea was freed from the Japanese colonialists in 1945, there were only half a dozen colleges and one university. Today there are more than 100 universities and colleges in South Korea alone.

In fact, the problem is of a reverse kind: South Korea produces more college graduates than it can properly employ and this has become a serious social problem. The country faces the same kind of problem with MBAs and other advanced degree holders. In addition to the hundreds of graduates South Korean universities send out each year, so many young people travel abroad in pursuit of higher degrees that the doctors of science, engineering and philosophy from France, Germany and the United States find themselves idle when they come home with their diplomas. North Korea also trains a large number of engineers, scholars and doctors.

The Koreans readily admit that their country is still far behind Japan and the advanced countries of the West, and that they have many problems. But they have no doubt that they will soon catch up. Koreans are proud that they have come so far so fast, and they don't want to settle for a second-class-citizen status.

CONFUCIANISM: THE CULTURE OF KOREA

진 How did Korea develop so fast against seemingly insurmountable odds? This is a question that many foreign scholars and governments have probed with intensity. Some of them concentrated on Korea's economic strategy. Others looked into its leadership. Still others studied the role of foreign capital. But the quest must start with the people and their culture. The people, after all, are what make a country.

What made the Korean advancement possible is the people's zeal for education and advancement. The Koreans, just as people in many other lands, take this ambition for granted because it is almost second nature to them; but it is a trait instilled in them by a long period of Confucian culture, particularly its respect for knowledge and for just authority.

Confucianism was introduced to Korea in the third century A.D. and became the state dogma under the Yi Dynasty (1392–1910). For centuries, the Korean elite prided themselves on mastering and following the teachings of Confucius. Even today, many Koreans refer to Korea as DONG-BANG YE-YI-JI KUK, the Eastern Nation of (Confucian) Decorum.

While Confucius is seldom mentioned — indeed, most young people would be surprised to learn that they are following Confucian teachings — the codes laid down by Confucius more than two thousand years ago still serve as the mainstay of Korea's social and ethical codes. This is true not only in South Korea but in Communist North Korea as well. An astute observer once referred to North Korea as a country under "Confucian Communism," and he was on the mark. Younger persons are expected to be deferential to their seniors in speech and behavior. For example, young men would not smoke in front of their seniors unless they were encouraged to do so.

AN OLD AND INDEPENDENT PEOPLE

진 The Koreans have been a proud people for centuries, though this may seem strange to some. Early Koreans built no empires. Neither did they build any pyramids, Great Walls or Colosseums. Although Korea was the first community in the world to use movable metal printing blocks, it made no earth-shaking contributions to science, technology or philosophy. Why, then, are the Koreans so proud of themselves?

Koreans take pride in their long history as an independent people with a culture and language of their own. They are proud of their uniqueness, their advanced civilisation and resilience. They take pride in the fact that they have surmounted overwhelming odds against them.

Given Korea's geographical and political location, its survival proves to be an accomplishment that is no small feat. Korea's location, more than anything else made it susceptible to many foreign invasions. The Korean peninsula protrudes southward from the northeastern corner of the Asian continent where many powerful tribes and nations emerged. It is surrounded on its other three sides by a large expanse of water. Not far from the southern tip of this small peninsula is Japan.

In the thirteenth century, when the Mongols were at their strongest, they wanted to dominate Korea. They also wanted to conquer Japan through the Korean peninsula. That Mongol invasion nearly obliterated all Korean identity.

In turn, the Japanese, in the sixteenth century wanted to take Korea as a land bridge through which they could attack China. Although Hideyoshi's forces bogged down in Korea because of fierce Korean resistance, Japan did finally succeed in taking over Korea in 1910 and used it as a base for continental expansion. Until their removal in 1945, the Japanese colonial government attempted to blot out all traces of the Korean nation, including its language. But the Koreans survived.

Its location played a key role not only in foreign invasions, but also in the physical make-up of the people, their culture and history. The Korean people trace their origins to the founding of the state of Choson by the mythical god-man, Tan'gun, in 2,333 B.C. on the banks of the Taedong River, located in the northwest of the peninsula. While many historians are dubious about the authenticity of the date or the man, there is a consensus that the kingdom of Choson was founded many centuries before Christ by the Yemaek tribe. This tribe was related to other tribes living in northern and northeastern China.

In 109–108 B.C. Emperor Wu Ti, "the Martial Emperor" of China, conquered the kingdom of Choson and ruled over it as a colony for four centuries. During that time Lolang, the core of the colony, became a great centre of Chinese art, philosophy, industry and commerce.

The year A.D. 53 brought about the emergence of the native kingdom of Koguryo. Koguryo carved out a vast domain in the northern part of Korea and Manchuria, now the northeastern region of China. The fall of the Han Dynasty in China and ensuing political chaos there enabled Koguryo to consolidate and extend its power, ousting the Chinese in 313.

In the middle of the third century A.D. two other kingdoms, Paekche and Silla, emerged in the southwestern and southeastern parts of the peninsula. Thus, the period between the third and the seventh century is known as the Three Kingdoms period. The period ended when the kingdom of Silla vanquished the others in 668, thus unifying the Korean peninsula. Korea remained a unified nation from then until 1945 when it was artificially divided into two parts by the United States and the Soviet Union.

After the Three Kingdoms period, Korea witnessed the rise and fall of three dynasties — Silla, Koryo and Yi. Each dynasty left its own marks on today's Korea. Hence it will be useful to review some of their distinguishing features.

The Silla Dynasty 668–932

The first two centuries of the United Silla Dynasty were marked by the establishment of new political, legal and educational institutions of considerable vigour. Domestic and foreign trade with Tang China and Japan prospered. Scholarship in Confucian learning, mathematics, agronomy and medicine also flourished. Buddhism, introduced to the peninsula in A.D. 372, reached its zenith.

Buddhism was naturally the dominant artistic influence. A number of bronze images of Buddha and the Bodhisattvas were made during the sixth, seventh and eighth centuries. The striking stone Buddha found in the Sokkuram, a cave-temple located near Kyongju in the southeast of the peninsula, was carved during the Silla Dynasty and is considered to be the finest of Korean stone carvings. Sokkuram is preserved today as a national monument and is open to public view. One should not, however, expect a replica of the larger-than-life Tunhuang. Sokkuram is best appreciated for its intricate design and beauty rather than for its scale.

During the centuries of Buddhism's ascendancy a large number of stone pagodas and temples were built also, one of the most famous being the Pulguksa (Buddhist Country Temple) near Kyongju, which was formerly the capital of Silla.

Silla, however, began to decline in the latter part of the eighth century. This eventually led to the emergence of the new Koryo Dynasty in 932 under a former general, Wang Kon.

The Koryo Dynasty, 932–1392

The founder of Koryo and his heirs consolidated control over the peninsula and strengthened political and economic foundations by more closely following the bureaucratic and land-grant systems of Tang China. The Dynasty witnessed nearly a century of thriving commercial, intellectual and artistic activities parallel to those of the Song Dynasty (960–1279) in China. Stimulated by the rise of printing in Song China, the Koryo Dynasty made great headway in printing and publication, leading to the invention of movable iron type in 1234 — two centuries before its use in Europe. Korea also became known during this time for its high quality paper, which is still treasured by the Chinese.

Buddhism continued to flourish under the Koryo Dynasty. Buddhist monks wielded overpowering influence in politics, the economy and the society during the latter part of the Koryo Dynasty. One of their most important accomplishments was the publication of Taejanggyong (Tripitaka Koreana), the most complete and best preserved of all the Buddhist scriptures. The original wooden plates for the 160,000-page text are still preserved at Haein-sa Temple near Taegu.

The Koryo Dynasty is best remembered for its celadons, or bluish-green porcelains, which are considered by many specialists to be the best in the world — surpassing even those made by the Chinese upon which they were originally modelled. Many have intricate designs of birds, flowers and other figures rendered in light and dark-coloured clay on the blue-green background, and some are delicately formed into the shapes of flowers, animals and objects. Many of these precious treasures can be seen in museums in Korea.

It should be noted also that it was the Koryo Dynasty which extended the country's northern border to the Yalu and Tumen rivers. The previous Dynasty's northern boundary was at the Taedong River about 100 miles further south.

The English word Korea comes from Koryo. Marco Polo, who visited China during the Mongolian dynasty of Yuan, referred to the country of Cauly, obviously using the Chinese pronunciation of Koryo which is Kaoli. For a long time, Westerners referred to Korea as either Corea or Coree.

By the twelfth century Koryo was plagued by internal and external problems. The situation was aggravated by the rise of the Mongols in the north, who launched a massive invasion in 1231. The Koryo armies put up fierce resistance but were no match for the highly organised mounted troops from the north, whose forces swept most of the known world during this period. The Mongols not only conquered Korea and China but most of what is now Europe and the Middle East.

Only in the early fourteenth century, when the Mongol empire began to disintegrate and the Ming Dynasty pushed the Mongols back to the north, did Koryo regain its independence. But the Dynasty was not to survive long. In 1392, it was replaced by the Yi Dynasty, headed by former general Yi Sung-gye.

The Yi Dynasty, 1392–1910

Yi Sung-gye founded the new Dynasty but called his kingdom Choson, reverting to the traditional name. The Chinese characters that make up the word Choson literally mean 'Morning Fresh' or 'Fresh Morning,' also translated as 'Morning Calm.' According to one noted Korean historian, the word Choson originally meant 'the beginning of dawn,' referring to the fact that Korea is the first place in the Asian continent to see the rising sun.

The end of the Koryo Dynasty also meant the end of Buddhist dominance. While a few of the monarchs in the Yi Dynasty were devout Buddhists, the dominant forces in the new Dynasty were Confucianists who regarded Buddhism as heresy. Accordingly, they launched a sweeping attack on Buddhist monks and institutions.

This was justified in part because the Buddhist temples had aggrandized large parcels of farm lands and exerted too much control over the politics and economy of the society. Because the temples' lands were exempt from tax rolls, the state became impoverished. In any event, the attack on Buddhism profoundly affected the character of civilisation on the peninsula.

Many of the outstanding temples were permitted to remain intact and some of the monarchs patronised them, but Buddhism exerted little influence over the religious life of Korea under the Yi Dynasty. Nor did any organised religion replace it. Korea effectively became a secular society.

Under this situation many people adhered to shamanism, geomancy, fortune telling and superstitions. Shamanism, or the belief in the spirits of objects in nature such as rocks, trees and mountains, is probably as old as human history, and the Yi Dynasty provided a fertile soil for it. Since nature was more powerful than man, many people worshipped the spirits of various objects and ancestors in times of distress. MUDANG, or the sorcerers, performed various rituals including songs and dances to appease these spirits.

(Confucianism, it should be remembered, is not a religion. It does not put forward the concept of a supernatural being to be worshipped. It is essentially an ethical doctrine governing human relationship and behaviour.)

The Koryo Dynasty fell partly because the Buddhists had too overpowering an influence. One can only speculate on the effect of having no organised religion under the Yi Dynasty.

THE CHINESE INFLUENCE

진 From the ancient period, Korea had very close ties with China and China exerted great influence on Korea's politics and culture. Korea of old was a tributary nation to China, whose emperor legitimised the new political leadership in Korea through investiture and received tributary missions. For the Koreans, the emperor in Beijing deserved reverence as a symbolic figure between heaven and earth, just as the Pope in Rome stands as a link between Christ and his followers.

While the Koreans genuinely respected China's great civilisation, the relationship between the two countries was also a means of ensuring Korea's existence and independence. Korea, on the one hand, had nothing to gain from a hostile relationship with China. For the Chinese, befriending Korea was a good way of guaranteeing tranquility in the neighbouring countries where its power did not reach. Since this relationship was cemented by the Confucian notion of duties and obligations, and served the interests of both parties, the bond lasted for centuries without much stress.

In the cultural realm, Buddhism, Confucianism and the civil service examination system were all imported from or through China. Hence Korean culture was similar in many ways to that of China.

So strong were the ties and similarities between China and Korea that, until the 1880s, elites of the past would have been proud to be regarded as a 'Little China.' But Koreans today would feel insulted by such a notion just as, for example, the Dutch would be offended by the suggestion that Holland is a Little Germany.

The Korean attitude began to change after China was conquered in 1644 by the Manchus, the barbaric tribe that originated in the immediate north of Korea. The Qing Dynasty (1644–1911) under the Manchus did receive Korea's homage because of its superior military power, but the emperor's legitimacy as the Son of Heaven was not fully accepted. Indeed, many Korean Confucians resented the Qing and continued to respect the Ming Dynasty.

China ultimately lost Korea's respect in the latter part of the nineteenth century when it tried to convert their traditional Confucian relationship into a naked imperial-colonial one and turn Korea into a Chinese colony. This was not what the Koreans anticipated from the suzerain. China became just another chauvinistic power, taking advantage of Korea's weakness. Very few Koreans bemoaned the Chinese defeat in 1895 by the Japanese.

The Japanese, however, had their own designs on Korea; Japan annexed Korea in 1910 and turned it into a colony.

JAPAN AND KOREA

With only two hundred kilometres between their nearest points, the Korean and Japanese peoples have had extensive contact since the beginning of their histories. Historians, in fact, have hotly debated the nature of that relationship in recent years.

As is the case in many relationships among close neighbours, the two peoples have not always enjoyed friendship. The Korean participation in Kublai Khan's abortive invasions of Japan in 1274 and 1281 did not help the situation much. Hideyoshi's

invasion of Korea between 1592 and 1598 devastated much of southern Korea, evoking bitter memories for a long time afterward. But the Tokugawa regime (1603–1868) in Japan actively sought friendly relations with Korea, and the Koreans dispatched twelve friendly missions to Japan between 1607 and 1811. Both countries were deeply imbued with Confucianism at that time, and this affinity served as a bond between the two equals.

The encroachment of the West in East Asia since the eighteenth century gravely affected the relationship between the two peoples. Japan not only sought to strengthen itself by emulating the West but decided on continental expansion as a means of strengthening itself against Western aggression. Korea became Japan's first step toward the continent. In spite of its long and proud history, Korea was not able to fend for itself; she and her people were forced to suffer humiliation at the hands of Japan. The reasons for this are manifold.

By the end of the nineteenth century, the Yi Dynasty was at the end of its dynastic cycle. Because the powerful families and Confucian academies did not pay tax in spite of their huge land holdings, the state was impoverished. The peasantry, constituting over 90 percent of the population, had to bear the brunt of the corrupt system, and many of them simply fled their farms.

Korea at this time was monolithic, rigid, self-righteous and exclusive. Its doors had been closed to all foreign countries for 300 years, except for China and occasionally Japan. Sure in the knowledge of Confucianism, the Korean literati rejected any idea that contradicted what they believed to be the truth. The prevailing orthodoxy could not be questioned or changed without a calamity. It was a proud, dogmatic and closed society that continued on in spite of itself. Soldiers were held in low esteem, and the literati neglected national defense.

Attempts were made by some reformists in the last decades of the nineteenth century to reorient the country, but it was not possible to reverse the floodtide of dynastic decay. The Yi Dynasty was doomed to fall and before the Koreans themselves could reset the course, the Japanese stepped in.

The generations of Koreans who lived under Japanese colonialism look back to those thirty-five years with anger and disgust. Far more than the Korean resources which the Japanese plundered from Korea, it is the humiliation inflicted by the Japanese that angers Koreans the most — their attempt to erase all Korean identity. In the 1930s and 1940s, the Japanese also exhausted the Koreans, both physically and mentally, by pushing them to serve the cause of the Japanese Empire in its Holy War against the United States, Britain and the Allies.

While thirty-five years is but a short period in Korea's long history, what happened during that period had a profound effect in later years. For one thing, the Japanese effectively destroyed the royal household, which was never to surface again. The leaders of Korea's resistance movement against Japanese colonial rule emerged as leaders of a liberated nation, free from the traditional leadership of earlier times.

The prolonged Japanese war against the Allies during World War II also brought the United States and the Soviet Union into Korea in 1945, which led to the division of Korea at the thirty-eighth parallel. The ensuing conflict between the two superpowers led to the establishment of two regimes with two capitals, one in Seoul and the other in Pyongyang — North and South Korea, no longer the united Korea of old.

This also proved to be the prelude to the Korean War that brought nothing but misery and destruction. That war officially ended with a truce in 1953, but two large and modern armies still confront each other at the truce line, ready to pull the trigger at a moment's notice. The reality of this is the frightening tragedy of it all. Who could know that the small group of men who met in Tokyo in 1937, plotting their strategies against China, or the other group planning an attack on Pearl Harbour in 1941 were instigating a chain reaction of such tremendous proportions?

The truce line in the middle of the Korean peninsula is today as impregnable as the Himalayas. For over three decades, not a piece of private mail has been exchanged over that line. Nor has a mortal crossed it to visit his or her relatives. Only in 1972 did the two sides begin to talk to each other, but the tension has not dissipated.

In September 1985, thirty-five persons from the South and thirty from the North crossed the line to embrace momentarily their long lost family members, but it has been impossible to arrange such a visit again. Those reunions were seen by tens of millions over television throughout the nation, and it is doubtful that anyone did not weep at the sight of their embraces. Tens of thousands of others have longed for nearly forty years to see family members on the other side of the truce line.

A BREATHTAKING LAND

진 The common feeling of being Korean comes not only from the shared history, language and customs, but also from the dramatic landscape that could only be Korea. The mountains of Korea are certainly a part of its people's identity.

Korea is a mountainous country, and they are seldom out of sight. "Over the mountains, mountains still, mountains without number" is an old saying.

Until recently, the spirits of the mountains were thought to walk about among the people. They were considered guardians of the living and of the dead. They skipped and danced, wept and laughed. They talked to the people in many persuasive voices. The mountains were part of the peoples' daily lives.

The most sacred of them all is Paektu-san or the White Head Mountain at the Chinese border. This is where the Korean ancestors were said to have originated; for centuries, even the hunters and sable trappers did not dare to intrude on the seclusion of the resident Spirit. The most ardent wish of the Korean is to visit the holy of holies, the volcanic crater on top of one of the peaks which has become a permanent lake known as Ch'onji or the Heavenly Lake.

Those who seek the most spectacular and grandiose of Korea's mountains must see the Diamond Mountains or Kumgang-san on the east coast, just north of the truce line. These are truly a gift from God to the Orient. He was in an extravagant and festive mood when he created them; he planted more than two thousand peaks on thousands of acres of land, each one different in shape and form. Some are exquisite in design, as if a fine jade piece. Others are of simple character. Some are grotesque and knotted; others are silky smooth. It was an artist of maturity who designed them.

There were Spirits here too, and in the olden days Buddhist monks in their monasteries placated them with prayers and offerings. Even today, a visitor can meet the SHIN-RYONG or the Spirits in these mountains. He sees them scattering the misty clouds around the peaks as the sun rises behind them. Quickly the clouds thicken to erase the whole scene. Another moment they lift the clouds to show the splendour of nature at its best. If you don't meet the SHIN-RYONG here, you are not likely to meet them at all.

The T'aebaek Mountain range, which includes the Diamond Mountains, continues southward to what is now South Korea, and one can enjoy the beauty of Sorak Mountain on the east coast, only a few hours' drive from Seoul. While the mountains themselves are not as spectacular as the Diamond Mountains, the scenery is beautiful. The fog and clouds moving in and out of the mountain paths are a veritable Oriental painting that one does not forget.

Spectacular sights can be seen all along the east coast. More often than not the mountains there are separated from the sea by precipitous cliffs, producing breathtaking sights. One can join the ranks of men and women who watched and breathed the dark blue water of the Eastern Sea for centuries from the tea huts or pavilions they built on choice spots on high ground.

A PHYSICAL PORTRAIT

진 Given their geographic proximity it is only natural that the Koreans, the Chinese and the Japanese share many common physical characteristics. One wonders whether even the natives of these countries could distinguish between themselves by physical features alone. Many natives would answer that they can, but because only a small minority of them have distinctive features they will fail more often than not when put to the test. If representatives of these three peoples were put in a neutral location, given identical clothing and haircuts, and made to sit quietly in a room, it would be difficult to tell them apart.

THE FAMILY UNIT

진 In earlier times, the honour and status of an entire family group depended on the academic performance of the children: the education of children was a family affair and they had a stake in the children's success.

Such pressure no longer exists, but the family remains the most important unit in Korean society, just as it is in other Confucian societies. Doing honour to the family is an important duty of the children. Carrying on the family name is also an important duty of the male offspring, and mothers without male children are pitied though no longer disgraced as in the past.

The Confucian principles governing the relationship within the family are very much alive. The father is master of the house, although he may not have the absolute sway on his wife and children he once did. Parents still do their utmost to push the children through the school system, and children are taught to honour and respect their parents.

Most Koreans still engage in ancestral worship. On Ch'usok, or Harvest Moon Day (August 15 in the lunar calendar), cemeteries are crowded with families paying homage to their ancestors. Wine and food are placed before ancestral tombs; children kneel in front of them and bow, the older ones first. Christians do not perform the ceremony, but they pay the annual homage nevertheless. It is the day for families to be united.

Korean names

Speaking of the importance of families in Korea, one must mention surnames. Foreigners will be struck by the fact that most of the people they meet are named either Kim, Lee or Park. This is because 45 percent of South Koreans (as of 1987) bear one of those names! To be more exact, 21.7 percent of Koreans (8,786,000, of them) are Kims, 14.8 percent are Lees and 8.5 percent are Parks. Other popular names are Choe (or Choy), Chung, Kang, Cho, Yun, Chang and Rim. These ten surnames comprise 64.5 percent of all the population's surnames.

How do the Koreans manage to distinguish each other? They manage because they refer to each other not by surnames alone, but by using the combination of surname and given name. While the people of other cultures use a limited number of given names, such as Bill or Jane, Ivan or Tanya, the Korean given names are as different from each other as are the constellations.

A LANGUAGE ALL ITS OWN

진 The Korean language is an important element of Korean identity, and a large part of what distinguishes Koreans from Chinese. I believe that, in spite of its many invasions and troubles, the Koreans maintained their national identity largely because of their distinct language. Had they not had their own language, Korea might have been absorbed by China or by one of the other numerous invaders. Korean culture survived the centuries of strong Chinese influence largely because the Koreans spoke their own language.

The Korean language, however, does show the heritage of Chinese influence. About 50 percent of all Korean words are loan-words from Chinese. For example, the Korean word for school is HAKKYO which is the Korean pronunciation of the Chinese word XUE-XIAO (pronounced SUEH-SHIAO). The Koreans simply took the Chinese word and pronounced it in the Korean way. The Japanese have done the same thing. The Japanese word for it is GAKKO. Indeed, the Korean government and the learned literati relied on the Chinese characters alone until 1910, although the Korean script, HAN'GUL, was invented in 1446.

To say that the Korean vocabulary is heavy with Chinese loan-words is not to say that the Korean language is the same or even similar to Chinese, just as English is not very similar to Latin in spite of the heavy dependence of English on Latin loan-words. Just as English-speaking people use loan-words from Latin or Greek without becoming self-conscious, the Koreans use Chinese loan-words inter-mingled with their own. For example, the common Korean greeting is "An-nyong ha-shim nika," or "Are you well?" AN-NYONG is from the Chinese word AN-NING meaning "in peace," but the rest is pure Korean.

In fact, the Korean and Chinese languages belong to different linguistic family trees. For one thing, the Korean language is not tonal like the Chinese one. A Korean without special training will not understand spoken Chinese even though he or she may grasp the gist of written documents. An ordinary Chinese listener would not be able to understand any Korean at all, written or spoken, because the Koreans now rely mostly on the Korean script, HAN'GUL.

Japanese belongs to yet another language family although the Korean and Japanese languages have many similarities, including grammar. The Korean and Japanese languages are rich in phonetic symbolism that enables one to express subtle nuances in states of mind and movements in nature, reflecting the subtlety and sophistication of these cultures.

The Koreans take much pride in their language for some good reasons. Theirs is the only language spoken inside its home country and not spoken as the first language anywhere else in the world. The Korean language belongs to the Koreans. While there are several dialects, Koreans understand each other without any difficulty even if they come from different parts of the country.

What makes them more proud, however, is the writing system. This is seen from the fact that Korea celebrates as a national holiday the day when HAN'GUL, the Korean vernacular script, was proclaimed — probably the only linguistic holiday in the world!

According to Professor Chin-W. Kim of the University of Illinois, Korean is one of the small number of the world's more than 4,000 languages that have writing systems specifically designed and invented for the language by a native.

HAN'GUL, an alphabetic and phonemic writing system, was invented in 1446 by King Sejong, the fourth monarch of the Yi Dynasty. Expert linguists regard it as one of the most elegant and most scientific writing systems in the world.

HAN'GUL is so simple in design that any student or foreigner who has learned the script can read any Korean material, though understanding the meaning is entirely another matter. The script employs fourteen consonant letters and ten vowel letters representing different sounds and these letters are combined in clusters to form a word.

Language, of course, tells much about a society and its culture. The Korean language has an elaborate honorific system which reflects the hierarchical nature of the Korean society. The Korean language prescribes different verbs and sometimes nouns, depending on who is speaking to whom or speaking about whom. Children may be told to PAP MOK-O, but the elder is told to TINJI JAPSU SEYO. Both are told to eat their dinner!

The honorific system is very intricate and cumbersome for foreigners to learn. Strangers talk to each other using the polite form, that is honouring each other. The older person in the family or in the work place talks down to the younger person while the younger one would use the polite form. There are many different shades of talking up and down. It depends on the degree of familiarity and intimacy.

RELIGION IN KOREA

진 Despite the attempts of the Yi Dynasty to eliminate the practice of Buddhism it proved too resilient. Its roots were too strong to be eradicated. The temples served as rallying points of the faithful, and it began to regain its following when the Dynasty was absorbed with other more urgent matters. The Japanese colonial administration also proved to be benign towards Buddhism because it was a religion the Japanese practiced.

Buddhism gained major impetus during General Park Chung Hee's presidency, from 1963 until 1979. Park was a devout Buddhist who was determined to restore Buddhism to its previous glory. Today, the largest number of religious South Koreans profess to be Buddhist.

Christianity also made its way into Korea in 1784 and played a major role in Korea's modernisation. Its attack against shamanism and superstitions has been largely successful. It also contributed to the propagation of HAN'GUL, because early missionaries saw this as the most effective way of propagating the Bible among the uneducated masses. It was through the mission schools that Western knowledge and that way of life was introduced and spread. Christians initiated the herculean task of liberating women from their traditional bondage and contributed to the abolition of class boundaries among the people.

The history of their martyrdom tells much about Korean Christians — but it also shows an aspect of Korean character that may not be readily seen. Korean Christians suffered gravely, first in the hands of Confucian-oriented native authorities and then under Japanese colonialists. They ran foul of Confucians because the Christians opposed ancestor worship. The Japanese also persecuted Korean Christians because they saw the church as a hotbed of Korean nationalism. Thousands suffered tortures and hundreds perished, but the church grew undaunted.

Today, 25 percent of the South Korean population profess to be Christians, either Catholic or Protestant. Not only are they present in large numbers, but their presence is conspicuous. In contrast to the Buddhists whose worship services are held in temples and monasteries far removed from metropolitan centres, Christians proclaim their presence through steeples, neon lights, early morning bells and store-front displays. The Full Gospel (Pentecostal) Church in Seoul has a membership of over 300,000 with a pastoral staff of over 100, and is the world's largest Christian congregation.

North Korea, on the other hand, is conspicuous for the absence of Christian churches. North Korean authorities insist that the hundreds of churches North Korea had before the Korean War were destroyed by American bombers, and there has been no attempt by the people to rebuild them. In any case, the authorities insist that there are congregations that are allowed to meet for Christian worship — though some outsiders think the reality of this statement's claim highly dubious. The constitution of the Democratic People's Republic of Korea guarantees religious freedom, but it also guarantees the right to oppose religious practice.

Korea also has an indigenous religion known as the Religion of Heavenly Way, or CH'ONDOGYO, which sprang up in late nineteenth century. It started as the TONG-HAK, or the Eastern Learning, pitching itself against Christianity — known at that time as Western Learning. The Tong-haks spearheaded a peasant revolt against corrupt officials in 1894, and established their roots in the countryside. Their doctrine is drawn from both Buddhism and Confucianism. Ch'ongdogyo now has 1.2 million believers and ranks third in size among religious groups in Korea.

EDUCATION

진 Like China during the same period, the Yi dynasty reinforced Confucian teachings through its civil service examination system. Mastering Confucian classics became the prime criterion for passing the examinations required for the elite to enter government service. And while government posts assured prestige, power and wealth, a family clan that did not produce examination passers within three generations was doomed to disgrace because the family would lose the status of yangban, the class that ruled over the farmers, merchants and artisans. Passing examinations, therefore, became a very serious family affair.

Education was a privilege only the rich could afford, but the value of education and learning came to be appreciated by all. The desire for better life, of course, is an instinct common to all human beings. So Koreans of all ranks pushed for education of the young as soon as the opportunity was available.

This opportunity was severely limited under the Yi Dynasty and the Japanese colonial period, but the situation changed abruptly after 1945, when Japan surrendered its control over Korea. There was a virtual explosion in the number of students in primary and secondary schools after 1945. The number of students attending colleges and universities also climbed sharply in both North and South Korea. It was this educated man- and woman-power that propelled Korea in its subsequent growth.

THE ARTS

진 Korean art expresses in yet another way the individual character of the country and people. Unlike the Chinese art forms, Koreans prefer simplicity and spontaneity. Korea is also too small to emulate the grandiose scale of Chinese art. One should not, for example, expect to find the mosaic of Buddhist statues of Tunhuang or Dazu in Korea. The simple forms, subdued colours and spontaneous expressions with a touch of humour which the Koreans prefer contrast dramatically to the grandeur, perfection and balance of Chinese art, which tends to be very detailed in design. Korean art also makes an interesting comparison with Japanese art which, is simple, yet, upon careful inspection, decorative and colourful.

Korea's geography and the harsh mountainous environment obviously affects its arts. In describing the characteristics of Korean art, Professor Kim touched on the essence of the Korean national character. She said: "Often Korean art displays carefree spirit and lack of technical perfection which is the result of unpretentious naturalism. Korean art also has human warmth and a certain degree of intimate naivete that invites the viewer to join the common aesthetic experience." It is no accident that traditional Korean furniture has attracted the attention of many Westerners attuned to modern art.

The key words here are 'carefree spirit,' 'unpretentious naturalism,' 'warmth' and 'intimate naivete.' These words aptly describe the Korean people themselves. I must quote our photographer, Mike Langford, who said in his letter from Korea in November 1987: "Like most of the Koreans I've met, they are warm and open and honest and giving!"

Koreans today do appreciate and enjoy their traditional art style, but this does not mean that they enjoy their form of art only. Western arts of various form and content are as popular in Korea as the traditional ones. There are probably more Western-style painters in Korea today than there are ones that practise the old form.

Koreans have been music lovers since ancient times. Song and dance festivals marked autumn harvests long ago. The music varies from the more sedate Confucian-temple and ancestral-shrine music to the animated NONG-AK, or the farmer's music, which accompanies the ribbon twirling and drum-beating movements of the dancers. The shamans, or sorcerers, also performed mask dances and puppet dramas to drive away evil spirits or to pray for the people's wishes. Professional singers told epic ballads to the accompaniment of drummers.

Koreans are avid fans of Western music too, from the classics to rock. 'Danny Boy' may be Irish in origin, but it is a part of most Koreans' repertoire.

CLOTHING

진 Koreans of the old days showed their preference for white clothing and they often referred to themselves as Paek-i minjok or, the nation clad in white clothes. According to a Korean scholar, it was because the Koreans considered themselves heirs of the sun, and because white represents the colour of the sun, that they wore white. In contrast, the overwhelming preference of the Chinese was the blue cloth.

Only rarely can one see these old costumes in the cities today. Western clothing has taken over as men's apparel in most of the cities, and the traditional costume is worn primarily on special occasions such as the New Year. One has to join the tourists and go to the Korean Folk Village (located thirty kilometres south of Seoul, just off the major highway) or the museum to see the wide-rimmed horse-hair hats, known as KAT, that were once the mark of Korean gentlemen. Many women still wear their traditional dresses, but colourful costumes are reserved for festive occasions. The long wide sleeves, banner-like ribbons for the blouse, baggy pants and the billowy skirts are simply too impractical for daily chores.

The Korean Folk Village was set up to replicate the way Koreans lived 200 years ago, before the country was 'corrupted' by Western ways. But this village is not the only place to see the Old Korea. Mike Langford, our photographer, visited one of these villages high on the eastern slopes of Chirisan National Park in the south central region of South Korea. There he found a village of TONG-HAK (or Eastern Learning) believers. The men were clad in white cotton clothes and wore their hair long. The unmarried men wore their hair in a plait and the married men wore it up under their hats — the elders of the village wore KAT, or horse-hair hats.

NORTH VERSUS SOUTH: THE RACE FOR DEVELOPMENT

North and South Korea entered the race for development in 1953, when the devastating war between them ended. It took leadership, good strategy and luck, however, to mobilise the available human and other resources for economic growth.

It appeared at first that Communist North Korea would win the race. North Korea had the advantage of hydroelectric generation stations and the foundation of the heavy industries built by the Japanese colonialists. The Communist system also seemed able to mobilise the resources of the country better. Kim Il-sung, the supreme leader of North Korea, solidified his political base after the war and launched a series of multi-year development plans that brought about impressive growth.

While North Korea did receive aid from its socialist allies, the people had to bear the major burden. The work they put in for economic reconstruction and development was stupendous. Since resources were scarce, whatever surplus the people produced was reinvested by the government for more growth. Consumption had to be minimised for the sake of higher production.

The North Korean government patterned not only its industrial development policy after that of Stalin's Soviet Union, but copied much of its agricultural policy as well. All the farms were collectivised between 1953 and 1958 to "lay the foundation for socialism." That socialism was what the leaders wanted to build.

But the communist system proved to have its limits. South Korea not only caught up with North Korea in the early 1960s, but began to outpace it. Indeed, South Korea attained one of the fastest growth rates in the world since the 1960s and transformed itself into one of the four Asian tigers.

South Korea's phenomenal growth since the late 1960s is due largely to the export-oriented industrial policy adopted by President Park Chung Hee, the president between 1963 and 1979. The former general's dictatorial rule caused much anguish and suffering for his opponents and critics, but his devotion to economic development paid its dividends. His unbending aim was to turn South Korea into an industrial country. Since few entrepreneurs had the capital to build factories, he encouraged them to borrow from abroad. He offered them support, protection and direction. Nothing was to hinder the building of factories that produced exportable commodities.

In time the country's technological level advanced and domestic savings increased. Fast-growing companies scoured the world for new markets. The world economy happened to be expanding when South Korea launched its export drive, and it was not difficult for the new entrepreneurs to find markets for their products.

The rapid economic development brought about a profound change in the attitude of the people. The two decades of success gave the people a confidence they had lacked. It also renewed the pride the people once had about their country — an invaluable boost because the Korean people's pride and confidence had been shattered since Korea was opened to the West in 1876. For a long time, the West appeared too advanced and too intimidating for the Koreans to hope to catch up. But, in the 1970s and the 1980s, the Korean perspective began to change.

While there are still pockets of poverty in South Korea, most of the people manage to enjoy a comfortable life. According to a survey conducted in 1987, over fifty percent of the people consider themselves to be in the middle class. 'Spring hunger', or the shortage of food among the farmers in the spring, was a chronic problem in Korea for centuries; the children of today learn about it only in history books.

THE DESIRE FOR UNIFICATION

진 Korea has been artificially divided into two parts for over forty years; and now, it seems, there is a strong contrast between the two countries. What the Allies called a temporary line of division "... to facilitate the disarmament of Japanese forces" turned into a blockade more rigid than any mountain range. A recent traveller remarked that "The North and South really do not meet any more, other than that they are both called Korea and they share a common geography and race."

While this dissolution may be the sad reality, Koreans on both sides of the dividing line long for the day when the barricades are removed and families reunited. The Koreans have made phenomenal progress in spite of the great losses they suffered during the Second World War, and in spite of all the resources and energy they wasted confronting each other during the Korean War. This ability to bounce back, in spite of such devastation, illustrates yet again the resilience and spirit of the Korean people. If they can remove the barricades that others erected within their nation, theirs will be a land of sixty million dynamic people making significant contributions to the world ahead. Judging by the stamina demonstrated over past centuries, that day may arrive sooner than anyone believes possible.

NORTH KOREA

We sat at the back of the train with our legs dangling out over the tracks as the train sped its way through the night back towards Pyongyang from Kaesong to the south. My fourteen day tour of the north was coming to an end and I had been feeling frustrated by the fact that I'd been allowed to photograph very little in the short time I had been permitted in the north.

Sitting there at the back of the train reflecting on it all, my guide was very sympathetic — though the system he supported would, at that point anyway, have had it no different — and so I too had to be understanding of the way it was. After all, the north had only just, for the first time since 1950, become open to westerners and in a way, I was lucky to be there at all.

In the dark of the night, watching the countryside rock past in a series of eerie silhouettes, my guide and newly found friend gave me a perspective that was to be the basis of this book of both North and South Korea:

"Over the centuries the Korean peninsula has been invaded countless times and even though we are separate today... we are both still, as we have always been, one people — Korean!"

6. Rice harvest on outskirts of Pyongyang

7. Main east/west highway, Pyongyang to Wonsan

8. Opera at Mansudae Art theatre, Pyongyang

9. *Following pages* The modern city of Pyongyang

10. Restaurant, east coast resort, Chongsokjong

11. Statues of socialist ideals, Pyongyang

12. Walking trail, Kumgansan area of Diamond Mountains

13. Water carriers, Kumgansan area

14. Hotel bell captain, Pyongyang

15. Traffic officer, Pyongyang

16. Village between Pyongyang and Wonsan

17. North Korean schoolgirls

18. Watching high-wire routine at Pyongyang Circus

20. Weekend artists abound in Diamond Mountains

19. Kuryong Falls, Diamond Mountains

21. Outside Pyongyang Indoor Sports Stadium

22. School children marching in downtown Pyongyang

23. One of the beautiful parks and gardens in Wonsan

24. Royal tombs from Koryo Dynasty, Kaesong

SOUTH KOREA
SEOUL REGION

I had been invited to attend a traditional Korean wedding at Korea House in downtown Seoul. It was a Saturday afternoon in early autumn and the trees were just starting to change colour. There was already a wedding ceremony being performed when I arrived — so I sat in a corner and watched, being careful not to intrude.

The ceremony was being performed in an open courtyard partly covered by a tent-like canopy that covered both the participants and the invited guests. Traditional music was being played and live chickens sat quietly in decorated baskets as was the way. During the ceremony every movement was studied and meticulously acted out, refined to a point of perfection by the passing of the centuries. The grace and beauty of it all was just stunning.

At the end of the ceremony the couple exited the courtyard and climbed a series of stone steps that led to a small house amidst some trees. I asked if I might follow them in order to see what was happening — permission was given so I followed, being very conscious of the fact that I was the only foreigner there. I found the couple sitting in a room, posing for photographs in their traditional Korean manner, behind a beautifully laid table of food.

I couldn't resist, and so stumbling my way through every apologetic Korean word I could mutter, and bowing in total humility, I entered the room and asked if I might also photograph them.

The groom smiled knowingly and replied in perfect English ''And what would our modelling fee be?'' . . . we all laughed and I took my photo, then left, having become the same rich colouring as the trees outside.

25. National Theatre, Seoul

26. Traditional wedding, Korea House, Seoul

27. Historical *Namdaemun*, South Gate of Seoul

28. Fan making, Suwon Folk Village, Seoul region

29. Suwon Folk Village duckpond

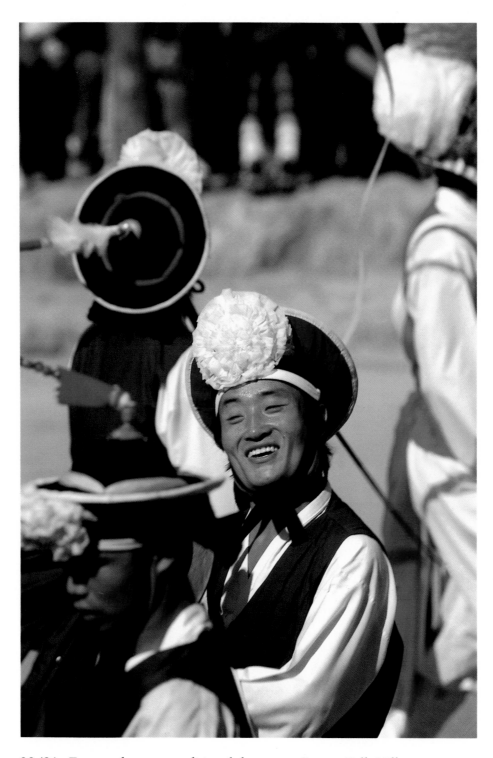

30/31. Farmers become traditional dancers at Suwon Folk Village

32/33.School children, Suwon

34. Drying grasses in sun, Suwon

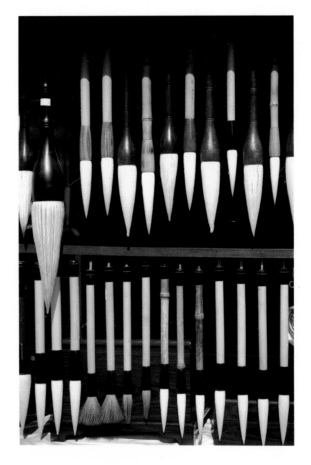

35. Calligraphy brushes,
Kyong-un-dong Antique Market, Seoul

36/37/38. Korean children

39. Musicians behind translucent screen, Seoul National Theatre

40. Fan dance, Seoul National Theatre

TANYANG AREA

Todamsambong is a very poetic Korean way of saying 'Three rocks in the River'. I'd seen a photograph somewhere of this place and decided that I should go there and see for myself what it was about. The photograph I'd seen was said to be of sunset... and so I went there for sunset.

But it turned out the caption was wrong and should have said sunrise. I stayed the night in the local town of Tanyang and rose at five the following morning so as to catch the first rays. It was late autumn and very cold. It was also very dark and I stumbled my way down to the water's edge — slipping and sliding my way over the frosty ground where I set up the tripod and camera and waited.

In the time before the dawn a dog arrived and sat with me — watching the subtle changes of light and colour as they worked their way towards daybreak. A car swung its way into the village behind where we sat, its headlights briefly illuminating the rocks and then plunging it all into darkness again. The dog raced off and barked at it a few times and then came back and watched some more with me. I learned later that he was the village guard dog.

It rained that morning and so there was no sunrise, and it was to be another month before I would return — by which stage ice had started to form around the base of the rocks in the river. The dog came and sat with me again and watched as I dragged a rowboat from down the river to place it in the photograph and create a visual harmony with the rocks and the two pavilions... and then my friend the guard dog and I sat and waited for the land of the morning calm to show herself to us.

42/43. Awaiting the bus, Andong

41. *Previous page* Todamsambong at sunrise, near Tanyang

44. Pulguksa Temple, Kyongju

45. Persimmons drying, Hahoe Village, Andong region

46. Foodstall in Andong market

47. Spreading fertiliser, Hahoe Village, Andong region

48. The last of the autumn harvest, Andong

49. *Following pages* Early morning cyclist, Andong

50. Traditional country house, Andong region

51. Chickchisa Temple

52. Andong farmers before autumn harvest work

53. Ploughing the traditional way, Hahoe Village, Andong region

54. Tombs of the Shilla Kings in the heart of Kyongju city

55. Stone pagoda, Mt. Namsan, Kyongju

56. Buddha of the Sokkuram Grotto, Kyongju

THE VILLAGE
OF THE
BLUE CRANE

"The sun was low in an autumn sky. The harvest had been gathered and sat patiently waiting to be threshed while the two farmers sat on the porch eating *kiwchi* and drinking rice wine.

I'd been watching them working most of the day but didn't feel I should intrude by asking if I could photograph — so I just sat and watched at a distance. It takes time and patience for people to accept you in these little villages but it's always rewarding in the end. The two farmers finally asked me over to join them in their eating and drinking and we sat together on the porch — communicating with smiles and gestures of friendship — our only common language.

We all ended up drinking too much and when it came time to work we were all quite hopelessly drunk and just fell about laughing.''

57. Outer Sorak, Soraksan National Park

58. Ice sledding a novel Korean way, Wontong

59. Ice fishing, Wontong

60. Inner Sorak mountains, Soraksan National Park

61. Naksansa Ulsanguae
Pavilion before sunrise, East coast

62. Naksansa Temple, East coast

63. Prayer beads, Chondungsa Temple, Kanghwado Island

64. *Following pages* Naksan Bodhisattva watches over the fishing fleet

65. Drying fish, Kanggu

66. A handful of squid, Kanggu

67. Alaska Pollack fish drying, Kanggu

68. Leftover harvest stubble provides a good fire, Kanggu

The Hallyo Waterway

The smoke from a passing coastal steamer hung like a signature in the blue grey of the early morning stillness of the waterway. I was on my way to Chungmu — a little fishing town on the south coast, having boarded the coastal steamer in Pusan earlier in the morning.

It was just my second day in South Korea and I was unsure of how things were, so just let things happen as they would. By mid afternoon I was becoming worried as to what had happened to my destination, as from the map it didn't quite look like it should have taken all this time.

Just while I was contemplating these thoughts a Korean deckhand came and gestured for my tickets — which I promptly handed him.

Humour and laughter (as I found out later) are very much a part of the Korean people — and this deckhand was having his fill. It appeared that we had passed through my port some four hours earlier and were now on the return leg and about to call there for a second time.

. . . and so the day was done and the waterway seen more fully than anticipated, and the photographer's journeys were started.

70. The port of Pusan is South Korea's second largest city

69. *Previous page* Coastal steamer between Pusan and Chungmu, Hallyo Waterway

71. Before dawn, Pusan fish markets

72. Portrait of schoolmaster, Chunghak-dong, Chirisan National Park.

73. Drying chillies, Chunghak-dong

74. Harvesting, Chunghak-dong

75. A cup of rice wine during a work break, Chunghak-dong

76. Traditional and modern ways combine for the harvest, Chunghak-dong

77. Andong villager returning from market

78. Chunghak-dong village elder

79. Young villager, Chirisan National Park

80. Farmer in The Village of the Blue Crane, Chunghak-dong

81. Bus departure at Chunghak-dong

82. Entrance bridge at Songgwangsa Temple

83. Traditional dress during harvest festival, Chunghak-dong

84. Grandfathers are Traditional
Village Guardians, Chejudo Island

85. Elders at Naejangsa Temple, Naejangsa National Park

86. Terraced farming, near Chungmu

87. *Following pages* Fishing nets in Naktonggang river estuary near Pusan

Technical Details

The cameras used were two Canon F1 bodies, a Canon 20mm F2.8 lens, Canon 28–85mm F4 zoom lens, Canon 100–200mm F4 zoom lens and Canon 300mm F4 lens — though most of the shots were taken either on the 20mm or 300mm lenses. A Metz CT45-5 flash was used as a fill in some instances as well as a gold reflector. The Film used was exclusively Kodachrome 64 ASA.

However — the most valuable element to this shoot was Anne Johnston, who joined me for one month in the south as an assistant and friend. Her presence and understanding helped me through the tough times — when nothing seemed to be going right and when I wasn't sure anymore as to the direction of the book — To her, we are indebted.

The Photographs

Cover: The *Honju* or master of ceremonies bows respectfully during a traditional Korean wedding held at Korea House in Seoul. Such wedding ceremonies are becoming more and more popular with young Koreans intent on retaining their traditional ways, while at the same time, adapting to the new demands of western culture.

End Papers: '1000 Buddhas depicting the life of Buddha as a child' as seen at Chickchisa Temple near Kimchon, South Korea.

Frontispiece: The traditional *Sam Taegeuk* tri-foliate design symbolising harmony among man, earth and heaven decorating a panel at Songgwangsa Temple, Chollanam-Do province, South Korea. This design is also the centrepiece of the South Korean flag.

2. A South Korean couple working in fields at the Suwon Folk Village south of Seoul. The village has been established to show traditional Korean lifestyles in a realistic working environment. The couple are tying up cabbages in order to protect them from early autumn frosts. The cabbages are used to make a traditional dish called *Kimchi*.

3. A statue of Kim Il Sung in the entrance hall of the Grand People's Study Hall, Pyongyang. Kim Il Sung is the President of the Democratic People's Republic of Korea (North Korea).

4. Early morning burn-offs fill a crisp autumn sky with smoke near Andong, while a local farmer wheels his cart along a river flood-bank on his way to a local market.

5. Bullrushes and ice-covered water reflecting a setting sun. Winter has arrived on the island of Kanghwado on the west coast of South Korea, near Seoul.

6. Rice harvest on the outskirts of Pyongyang. During the height of the harvest, busloads of students and office workers travel daily into the countryside to help bring in the crops.

7. The new east-west highway between Pyongyang and Wonsan, North Korea.

8. A socialist inspired opera being performed at the Mansudae Art Theatre in Pyongyang, North Korea.

9. The modern city of Pyongyang as seen from the top of the Tower of Juche Idea. Most of this city was rebuilt in 1953 at the end of the Korean War.

10. A portrait of Kim Il Sung hangs on a dining room wall at the east coast beach resort of Chongsokjong. Such portraits are found in all public areas throughout North Korea.

11. Statues reflecting socialist ideals stand at the foot of the Tower of Juche Idea in Pyongyang.

12. A walking trail high in the Kumgansan National Park. This park is part of the fabled Diamond Mountains that are featured in the folklore of both North and South Korea.

13. Women carry water pitchers on their heads in the traditional manner in the Kumgansan area. It seems that such traditional portage methods are frowned on by the authorities in the north, as on many occasions, womenfolk in the north would see me coming and would take their loads off their heads until I had passed by.

14. A highly decoratively uniformed Bell Captain at the Koryo Hotel in Pyongyang. The Koryo is the newest and largest hotel in the city — comprised of twin towers each 45 storeys high.

15. A traffic officer working point duty in downtown Pyongyang. Her movements were so precise and clocklike that I stood mesmerised by her actions for quite some time — oblivious to the crowd that in turn had stopped to watch me.

16. Thatched roofs of a traditional village near the east-west highway between Pyongyang and Wonsan.

17. Schoolgirls at a Pyongyang all-girls school.

18. School children watch with bated breath as an acrobat does her routine on the highwire at the Pyongyang Circus.

19. The famous Kuryong Falls in the Kumgansan Mountains. These falls are portrayed in traditional North Korean paintings, tapestries and embroideries.

20. Artists enjoying a weekend out in the valleys of the Kumgansan Mountains.

21. Athletic sculptures in the socialist tradition outside the National Indoor Sports Stadium in Pyongyang.

22. School children marching and singing socialist songs in Kim Il Sung Square, Pyongyang. Their singing is a constant sound in the city as groups of children march their way to and from the museums and art galleries.

23. A beautiful park setting in the east coast city of Wonsan.

24. Royal Tombs dating from the Koryo Dynasty of the 10–14th centuries near Kaesong — which was at that time the capital of Korea.

25. Traditional music being performed at the National Theatre in Seoul.

26. A newlywed couple at a table laden with delicacies after their traditional wedding ceremony at Korea House, Seoul.

27. The Namdaemun Gate (South gate) is Korea's number one national monument. The gate is one of four gates that traditionally were part of the city walls of ancient Seoul.

28. Fan-making in the traditional manner at Suwon Folk Village south of Seoul.

29. A duck pond at the Suwon Folk Village.

30. The traditional Farmer's Dance being performed at Suwon Folk Village.

31. Dancers returning from a performance at Suwon Folk Village.

32/33. School children wearing identical clothes and bags.

34. Grasses drying in the sun at Suwon Folk Village.

35. Calligraphy brushes on display in the window of a fine arts shop in the Kyong-un-dong antique market in Seoul. Korea is reknowned for its calligraphic art.

36/37/38. Korean Children.

39. Musicians play behind a large hanging translucent screen, visually reiterating the background nature of their music, during a traditional dance performance at the Seoul National Theatre.

40. Vibrant colour in a scene from the 'Fan Dance' at the Seoul National Theatre.

41. A rowboat moored at Todamsambong near Tanyang. Todamsambong is the Korean name for the three rocks in the river.

42. An elderly woman patiently waits for her local bus in Andong.

43. Also waiting for his bus, a grandfather enjoys a quiet smoke — Andong.

44. Autumn colour fills the trees at Pulguksa Temple near Kyongju.

45. Persimmons drying under the eaves of a traditional Korean dwelling in Hahoe Village near Andong.

46. A food stall in the Andong market.

47. A villager spreads fertiliser by hand in the village of Hahoe. Hahoe is one of many villages in South Korea that still adhere to traditional ways.

48. A farmer ties up the last of his harvest before transporting it to market in the Andong region.

49. An early morning cyclist travels a country road on his way to market, Andong region.

50. Traditional styled country house near Andong.

51. Autumn colours at Chickchisa Temple.

52. Farmers warm their hands before starting work during a late autumn harvest near Andong.

53. Traditional methods of ploughing are still used in many isolated areas in the south.

54. Tombs of the Shilla Kings in the heart of the city of Kyongju. This city is referred to as a 'museum without walls' because of its many historic sites.

55. An ancient stone pagoda on the slopes of Mt. Namsan near Kyongju.

56. Buddha of the Sokkuram Grotto near Kyongju.

57. Under a blanket of rain and low cloud the autumn colours of Outer Sorak in Soraksan National Park are spectacular.

58. This was the first time in all my Asian travels that I had seen such an 'ice sled' propelled by two sticks with nails at the ends. This winter activity was popular with children throughout South Korea.

59. Ice fishing is a popular winter sport in South Korea. This man was a little shy when I asked if I could photograph him — it could have had something to do with the tiny fish on the end of his spear — near Wontong.

60. There is a stark graphic beauty to the Inner Sorak Mountains in early winter that is uniquely Korean — Soraksan National Park.

61. Naksansa Ulsanguae Pavilion just before sunrise. This pavilion is located on the north east coast of South Korea where the mountains are very close to the sea — making the scenery especially spectacular.

62. The first rays of the morning sun reflect off a gold Buddhist motif at Naksansa Temple.

63. A priest holds his prayer beads behind his back while in conversation at Chondungsa Temple on Kanghwado Island.

64. The Naksan Budhisattya watches over the fishing fleets like a guardian angel.

65. Hardy womenfolk spend their days endlessly tying up fish for drying, in the east coast fishing village of Kanggu.

66. A young girl scoops up a handful of squid at Kanggu.

67. Alaska Pollack fish laid out for drying at Kanggu.

68. Children sit and watch as a farmer burns off stubble left over from the harvest at Kanggu.

69. A coastal steamer plies the waterway between Pusan and Chungmu in the Hallyo Waterway.

70. Pusan — a busy port and second largest city in South Korea.

71. Every morning before dawn the Pusan fish markets are a hive of commercial activity.

72. Portrait of the schoolmaster at Chunghak-dong (known as The Village of the Blue Crane) — a traditional community upholding ancient religious beliefs. As a respected elder of the village he wears the traditional black horse-hair hat known as a *Kat*.

73. Chilli peppers laid out to dry at the village of Chunghak-dong.

74. Bringing in the harvest in a traditional manner, Chunghak-dong.

75. Farmers enjoying a break and a cup of rice wine or *Makkulli*, Chunghak-dong.

76. Even in villages of traditional ways, modern machinery is an integral part of the harvest, Chunghak-dong.

77. A villager returns from market well laden in the Andong region.

78. The village elder takes a late afternoon stroll in the village of Chunghak-dong.

79. Dressed in traditional whites with his hair in a single long braid, a young villager of Chunghak-dong sits high on a ridge above the village in Chirisan National Park. Tradition holds that unmarried men of the village wear a single braid until marriage, when it is wound into a topknot. Their hair is never cut.

80. A young farmer, Chunghak-dong.

81. Chunghak-dong villagers paying their respects to a relative departing on a bus from their remote village after the 'harvest festival'.

82. A tranquil setting at Songgwangsa Temple — a bridge spans a stream to the temple entrance. This is the centre of Son Buddhism (the Korean form of Zen) and one of the three largest temples in Korea.

83. A young girl wearing traditional dress during the long weekend of the 'harvest festival' at the village of Chunghak-dong.

84. *Tol-harubang*, or grandfather stones — the mysterious carved lava statues of Chejudo Island. These quizzical fellows are thought to represent legendary guardians of the township of Chejudo.

85. Three elders watching something, (I looked but couldn't see anything anywhere, even though they were looking like this for some time), Naejangsa Temple in Naejangsa National Park.

86. Terraced farming around a small village near Chungmu.

87. Fishing nets in the Naktonggang river estuary near Pusan.

MIKE LANGFORD is a New Zealander, based in Sydney,
working out of the Rapport Photo Agency.

He is an indefatigible worker, an extensive traveller
and has photographed for many notable volumes, including 'Han Suyin's China' and 'A Day in the Life of New
Zealand'. His work also appears in many periodicals.

The winner of many professional photographers' gold
awards, he is a great companion and conversationalist
— a publisher's delight!